Unlikely Partners

by Marilyn Shimkus

Harcourt
SCHOOL PUBLISHERS

Cover, ©PhotoDisc/PunchStock; p.3, ©Shirley Vanderbilt/Index Stock Imagery; p.4, p.7 ©Corbis; p.5, ©Fred Bavendam/Minden Pictures; p.6, ©FRED BAVENDAM/Minden Pictures; p.8, (l) ©Peter Johnson/CORBIS, (r) ©Corbis; p.9, ©Alex Wild/Visuals Unlimited; p.10, ©PIOTR NASKRECKI/ Minden Pictures; p.11, ©FRANS LANTING/Minden Pictures; p.12, ©Eric and David Hosking/CORBIS; p.13, ©Reinhard Dirscherl/Visuals Unlimited; p.14, ©Zigmund Leszczynski/Animals Animals.

Printed in China

ISBN 10: 0-15-350518-4
ISBN 13: 978-0-15-350518-8

Ordering Options
ISBN 10: 0-15-350334-3 (Grade 4 Below-Level Collection)
ISBN 13: 978-0-15-350334-4 (Grade 4 Below-Level Collection)
ISBN 10: 0-15-357508-5 (package of 5)
ISBN 13: 978-0-15-357508-2 (package of 5)

2 3 4 5 6 7 8 9 10   985   12 11 10 09 08 07

A large grouper fish swims up to a coral reef. Tiny crustaceans, or shelled animals, are stuck to the grouper. The fish waits for a few minutes. Soon a yellow cleaner wrasse swims up to it. The grouper, which is much larger, does not attack the cleaner wrasse. Instead, it lets the cleaner wrasse come close. When the cleaner wrasse is close enough, it begins to eat the crustaceans off of the grouper.

This is an obvious example of one fish helping another. The grouper gets rid of the crustaceans. The cleaner wrasse gets plenty to eat.

Grouper fish

3

There are many other examples of how living things help one another in nature. Most often, organisms, or living things, that have very different needs pair up.

Tiny organisms called bacteria live in the stomachs of cattle. The cattle eats grass. The bacteria then "eat" the grass in the cattle's stomach. This helps the cattle digest the grass.

Bacteria and cattle are two very different organisms. They live in very different ways. They have very different needs, yet they help each other.

Red hermit crabs live off the coast of North America. Hermit crabs do not have their own shells. They find empty shells, and then they live in them. As the hermit crabs grow, they find larger shells in which to live.

Sea anemones are colorful animals that live in oceans. Their bodies are shaped like tubes. Tentacles surround their mouths. They often use the tentacles to sting predators. Most anemones do not move. They just stick themselves to a rock or shell.

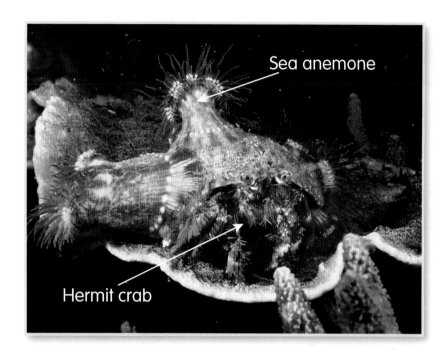

Sea anemone

Hermit crab

Some red hermit crabs and sea anemones help each other. An anemone may stick to the crab's shell. The hermit crab allows this. Now predators will avoid the crab. This is because they do not want to get stung by the anemone. By letting the anemone stay on its shell, the crab is protected.

The anemone is also helped. Riding on the hermit crab makes it possible for it to move from place to place. This gives the anemone a better chance of finding food. Also, it gets to eat the hermit crab's leftovers.

A giraffe walks across the plains of East Africa. It stops at an acacia tree. The giraffe pulls leaves off of the tree and eats them.

Then a gray bird with a red beak comes up. It seems to be lured to the giraffe's long neck. The bird lands on the giraffe's neck. The giraffe does not try to make the bird leave.

The bird is a red-billed oxpecker. Sometimes it is called a tickbird. It's called that because it eats ticks. Ticks are small insects. After landing on the giraffe, the oxpecker uses its beak like a scissors to cut through the giraffe's fur. This trait allows it to find and eat ticks, fleas, and flies. The bird is happy because there's plenty of food.

The giraffe is happy, too. The oxpecker helps it get rid of insects. Also, the oxpecker makes a loud hissing sound when it is scared. This hiss tells the giraffe that a dangerous animal may be coming. This helps both the oxpecker and the giraffe.

Most types of acacia trees have chemicals in their leaves that make the leaves taste bad. This protects the trees from the damage that insects and animals could cause. It helps the trees live longer.

The bullhorn acacia doesn't have these chemicals. It depends on a certain type of ant to protect it. The ant is called an acacia ant. It lives in the bullhorn tree.

The bullhorn acacia makes sweet liquid that the ants eat. This liquid helps the ants grow larger. In order to protect their home and food, the ants attack anything that comes near the tree. They attack animals and other insects. They also attack plants that grow near the base of the tree. This gives the bullhorn acacia tree more sunlight. It also helps the tree get more of what it needs from the soil.

The ants protect the tree. The tree gives food and shelter to the ants.

Another example of animals helping each other is the Egyptian plover bird and the crocodile. These are animals that live in Africa. The Egyptian plover bird helps the crocodile by eating parasites off of the crocodile's body. Parasites are organisms that would hurt the crocodile. The crocodile will even allow the plover bird to go into its open mouth in order to remove the parasites from in there!

The Egyptian plover bird is also helped by this relationship. The bird gets all it needs to eat. It is also very safe because no animal is going to bother another animal that is sitting on the back of a crocodile!

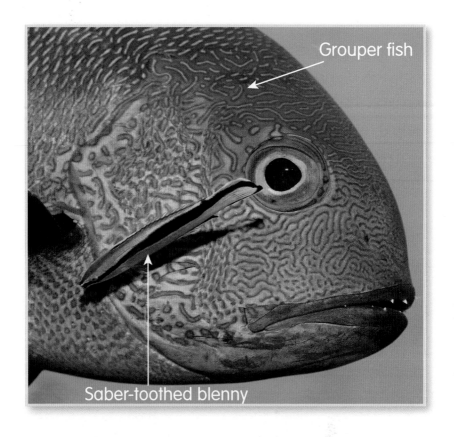

Grouper fish

Saber-toothed blenny

Sometimes only one animal benefits from its relationship with another. Remember how the barberfish and grouper fish helped each other? There is another fish that uses this relationship to meet its own needs. It is called the saber-toothed blenny. The blenny resembles another fish called a cleaner wrasse in both the way it looks and acts.

The deceptive blenny swims up to the grouper fish. The blenny mimics, or acts like, it is a cleaner wrasse. The grouper thinks the blenny is going to help it by eating the crustaceans off its side.

The blenny is not there to help the grouper, though. When the blenny is close enough, it attacks the grouper fish. Often the blenny takes a bite right out of the grouper's fin! The grouper has been tricked. Hopefully, the grouper won't get scared when a real cleaner wrasse comes around again!

Think Critically

1. Why do acacia ants protect bullhorn acacia trees?

2. How do bacteria help cows?

3. What word means almost the same thing as *mimics* does on page 14?

4. Why do you think a barberfish is named that?

5. What are some details from this book that interested you?

 Science

Find Out More Choose an animal that is mentioned in this book. Look in a science book or the Internet, and find three more facts about that animal. Write the facts on a note card to share with the class.

School-Home Connection Discuss this book with a family member. Then have a discussion about how plants and other animals help humans.

Word Count: 932 (943)